VIKTOR E. FRANKL

AND THE SEARCH FOR MEANING

VIKTOR E. FRANKL

AND THE SEARCH FOR MEANING

21 Reflections on Living Life with Purpose

A COMPANION

PAM ROY *and* MOIRA HUMMEL

Foreword by ALEXANDER VESELY-FRANKL

Beacon Press, Boston

BEACON PRESS
Boston, Massachusetts
www.beacon.org

Beacon Press books are published under the auspices of
the Unitarian Universalist Association of Congregations.

28 27 26 25   8 7 6 5 4 3 2 1

This book is printed on acid-free paper that meets
the uncoated paper ANSI/NISO specifications for
permanence as revised in 1992.

Cover and text design by Carol Chu

Library of Congress Cataloging-in-Publication Data
is available for this title.
ISBN: 978-0-8070-1871-2

FROM PAM

For my daughters,
Emily, Rachel, and Allison,
and youth everywhere
yearning to discover
meaning in their lives.

FROM MOIRA

For Brian, Becky, Joe, Tori,
Jessica, Noah, Kathy, and
my parents with many thanks
for your love and support.

CONTENTS

FOREWORD
BY ALEXANDER VESELY-FRANKL,
GRANDSON OF VIKTOR FRANKL   1

INTRODUCTION   5

REFLECTIONS
ONE: PURPOSE   11
TWO: LIVING   19
THREE: HAPPINESS   25
FOUR: REACTIONS   31
FIVE: TOLERANCE   39
SIX: COMMUNITY   49
SEVEN: SELF-TRANSCENDENCE   57
EIGHT: BE THE CHANGE   63
NINE: HUMOR   71
TEN: UNIQUENESS   79
ELEVEN: HUMANITY   85
TWELVE: FREEDOM   95
THIRTEEN: MONEY   103
FOURTEEN: EMPTINESS   111
FIFTEEN: RESPONSIBILITY   121
SIXTEEN: HUMAN SPIRIT   125
SEVENTEEN: TENSION   133
EIGHTEEN: SOLITUDE   145
NINETEEN: SUFFERING   155
TWENTY: WORK   165
TWENTY-ONE: CHOICES   175

ACKNOWLEDGMENTS   191

SOURCES   193

MORE INFORMATION   195

ABOUT THE AUTHORS   199

FOREWORD

Many people are familiar with the name of my grandfather, Viktor Frankl, but few know much about his message. He is often recalled as a Holocaust survivor, but in reality, that experience played a small role in his overall life's work. His greatest contribution to humanity was recognizing meaning as a central factor in mental health.

My grandfather's interest in psychology started at an early age. He enrolled in adult night classes when he was in junior high school. His first article was published when he was eighteen, and by the time he was twenty-two, he was lecturing on the meaning of life. In 1930, at the age of twenty-five, he organized youth counseling centers in Vienna, successfully combatting the epidemic of teen suicides that would occur around the time report cards were issued. Within a year, suicides dropped to zero. By the time he completed medical school, he had developed a specialty in psychiatry and neurology with a focus on treating suicidal patients.

His views about meaning brought him into conflict with Sigmund Freud and Alfred Adler, the founders of modern psychotherapy. As a teenager, he corresponded with Freud, and then joined Adler's school for a time. While my grandfather acknowledged the importance of their work, he went on to establish his own theory, which is often referred to as the third Viennese school of psychotherapy. He named the theory logotherapy, from the Greek for "healing through meaning."

Years before World War II, he treated thousands of suicidal patients at psychiatric hospitals and developed the core principles of logotherapy. The completed manuscript of his first book about it was confiscated when he was sent to Auschwitz. He was thirty-seven years old at the time. His encounters with the worst of human conditions ended up providing him with an unwanted laboratory that confirmed his theory. He saw that those who were oriented toward a meaning to be fulfilled were more likely to survive.

After the war, he taught throughout the United States and held professorships at Harvard, Stanford, Southern Methodist University, and Duquesne University in Pittsburgh. The English translation of his book *Man's Search for Meaning* was published in 1959 and became an international bestseller. My grandfather saw this not so much as a personal achievement but as a symptom of the mass neurosis of modern time, since its title promised to deal with the question of life's meaningfulness. Decades later, the book still shows up consistently on Amazon's top 100 books.

Logotherapy as a psychological practice is hard to standardize, package, and market, so it has not gained as much traction in the United States as it has in other parts of the world. It recognizes that every person is unique and cannot fit into a standardized theory. Requiring creativity and flexibility, therapy at its best is as much an art as a science. He liked to refer to American neurologist George M. Beard, who noted that if two cases of neuroses were treated the same way, at least one was treated improperly.

I was lucky enough to grow up knowing my grandfather both personally and professionally. He encouraged my love of film-making when I was a teenager and also supported my decision to become a logotherapist when I was an adult. I have had the privilege to archive innumerable videos and interviews of him throughout his life. These are constant reminders of his timeless wisdom and his wonderful sense of humor—another quality he believed to be a resource of healing and well-being.

I met Pam and Moira while we were working together on a film project. Friends for over forty years, they were inspired to write this thought-provoking book about meaning because of their concern for America's youth and the growing epidemic of mental illness. They recognize the importance of my grandfather's philosophy of life and have used it to guide their own lives and raise their children. Just as he did, they see the bigger picture, the underlying problems, and the systemic issues that need to be addressed. My grandfather would be pleased that they are introducing his ideas to a new generation of readers.

—*Alexander Vesely-Frankl*

INTRODUCTION

"People may have enough to live by; but more often than not they do not have anything to live for."

As human beings, we are motivated to find meaning. However, meaning is unique to each person. It cannot be created or given to us—it must be discovered. Our search for meaning is a personal journey that each of us must take. This book encourages that journey. Through inspiring quotes from Viktor Frankl and accompanying exercises for self-discovery, it offers twenty-one reflections on topics such as purpose, freedom, and self-transcendence. These reflections can be contemplated over twenty-one days or twenty-one years. They can be done in any order and revisited at any time. They simply create space for you to become more aware of who you are and how you fit into the world. Life has meaning under all circumstances, including the most undesirable. Even if our only source of meaning is our attitude toward an unavoidable situation, we have the freedom and responsibility to answer the demands life presents to us. No matter where you are in your life, this book facilitates the search for meaning, which is our primary motivation for living.

The life and work of Viktor E. Frankl (1905–1997) inspired this book. From the time he was a young boy, Frankl believed that meaning was central to life.

As a neurologist and psychiatrist, he studied it. As a philosopher, he sought to understand it. As a survivor of concentration camps during the Holocaust, he lived it. Frankl's life journey showed him that "he who has a *why* to live can bear almost any *how*." This statement by Friedrich Nietzsche anchored Frankl's belief that discovering our *why*—the meaning we attach to our lives—is essential to our health and well-being.

Before the onset of World War II, Frankl had developed a theory called logotherapy, which literally means "healing through meaning." His extensive university training, combined with his experiences working in suicide clinics and living in concentration camps, reinforced his theory. While logotherapy is a form of psychotherapy (part of humanistic and existential psychology), it is also a philosophy for life, focusing on meaning, freedom, and responsibility. For the purposes of this book, we use its guidance as a life philosophy rather than for its clinical application.

Over a nine-day period following the war, Frankl wrote his best-selling book, *Man's Search for Meaning*. According to a 1991 survey by the Library of Congress, the book is considered "one of the ten most influential books in America." The first part of the book describes the horrors of the Holocaust, when Frankl lost his parents, his brother, his wife, and his unborn child. The second part introduces and explains logotherapy, which focuses on what is right with us, our humanity and our meaningful futures. *Man's Search for Meaning* has inspired millions around the world.

Logotherapy recognizes the interrelationship of the mind, body, and spirit. It teaches that there is a spiritual dimension to being human that is alive and well in each one of us. This "human spirit" gives us the ability to step outside ourselves and reflect on our lives, provides us with goals and direction, and generates freedom of choice. It is what distinguishes us from other mammals—not falling under the umbrella of any religion but instead representing the essence of our humanness. Our human spirit is always healthy and has vast untapped resources. When we ignore or suppress it, we can become distressed. Throughout time, the defiant power of our human spirit has inspired our evolution. It is constantly striving to push us forward, from who we are to what we can become.

When our search for meaning is denied or ignored, we experience an inner void that Frankl termed an "existential vacuum." It is this vacuum that can lead to anxiety, depression, aggression, addiction, and even suicide. We can see the telltale signs of this existential vacuum everywhere in our culture, affecting all ages, races, and socioeconomic levels. Every era has its own collective neurosis, and this existential vacuum is ours.

Like all humans at any time, we want to avoid the suffering caused by guilt, pain, and death—the "tragic triad" that Frankl explains is part of being human. For Frankl, suffering is not the same as despair—despair is suffering without meaning. Suffering is unavoidable. Despair involves choice. Indeed, our resistance to examining our suffering for meaning leads to despair, which, in part, results in the epidemic levels of self-harm, addiction, mental illness, and suicide.

Our culture's current focus on the pursuit of happiness is actually one of the causes of our existential vacuum and feelings of despair. We feel ashamed if we are unhappy, as if it were a disease. It is not possible to be happy all the time; it is an unattainable goal. Life brings with it some unavoidable, unhappy experiences. The choices we make and how we deal with these times give our lives meaning and, thus, fulfillment. Frankl's work shifts our focus away from the naïve pursuit of happiness to the mature pursuit of meaning.

As you will discover through the reflections to come, meaning is all around us and available to us at any moment. It can be found through:

- making a difference in the world through our actions, our work, or our creations
- experiencing something (truth, beauty) or encountering someone (love)
- adopting a courageous and exemplary attitude in situations of unavoidable suffering

As humans, we are characterized by our spirituality, our freedom, and our responsibility. But too often, we choose not to take responsibility for ourselves. We want someone else to be responsible for us, to provide us with certainty in an uncertain world. We like to turn over responsibility to corporations, governments, schools, churches, and even medical professionals. But finding and fulfilling meaning is our personal task, not something we can delegate.

Each of us is unique and irreplaceable. That existential void we feel is real and an affliction of our time. However, reaching into that void to discover meaning will free us to become who we are meant to be. The philosophy of logotherapy teaches responsibility as the cornerstone of freedom. It seeks to prevent spiritual distress and the resulting mental illnesses with a focus toward the future and our unique role in shaping it.

Most of all, logotherapy encourages us toward self-transcendence, the ability to share our authentic self with others to better a worthy cause or to love another. This is the highest goal of human beings, and it has the power to change the world.

"A human being is not one thing among others; things are determining each other, but man is ultimately self-determining. What he becomes, he has made out of himself. In the concentration camps, e.g., in this living laboratory and on this testing ground, we were watching and witnessing one part of our comrades behaving like swine while others were behaving like saints. Man has both potentialities within himself; which one is actualized depends on decisions but not on conditions."

PURPOSE

"A man* who becomes conscious of the responsibility he bears toward a human being who affectionately waits for him, or to an unfinished work, will never be able to throw away his life. He knows the 'why' for his existence and will be able to bear almost any 'how.'"

We need to know we matter in the world, that there is a place for our uniqueness, and that what we have to contribute cannot be offered by anyone else. When we believe we are no more valuable than a manufactured widget, suicide can feel like a reasonable option. This feeling of despair happens when we lose sight of our distinct contribution to the tapestry of life.

Mark Twain said, "The two most important days of our life are the day we are born and the day we figure out why." We are invaluable to the world—we all have a purpose for being here. Purpose is something

---

*Befitting the era of his writing, Viktor Frankl used "man" to refer to humankind—it is not related to gender.

we discover, and for each person it is different. We can find it only in the context of our lives—through our contributions, our relationships, our experiences, and our attitudes. Purpose is not about tallying up individual achievements. Purpose is about consciously forging our own path. It involves listening to our conscience, trusting its guidance, and taking action. When we are able to see the many meaningful moments we create and experience, whether they are big or small, we will not throw away our life. We recognize our significance and importance.

Reflect on your relationships, your contributions, or your experiences in the last month. Identify one or more instances where your presence made a difference, big or small. What unique characteristics or contributions did you make?

How did your presence make a difference?

Looking around you today, what tasks that need to be done could use your unique abilities?

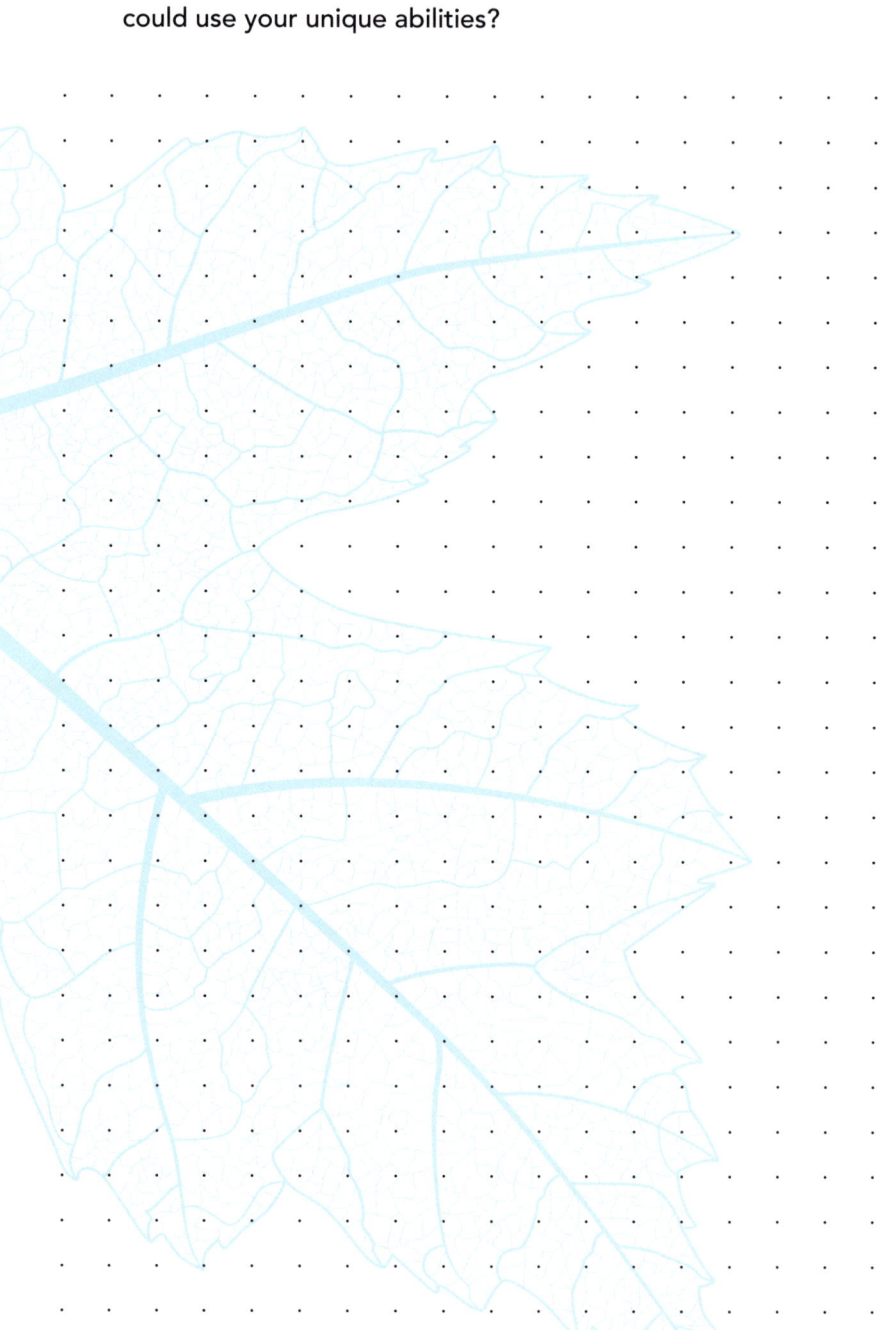

LIVING

"A life of short duration . . . could be so rich in joy and love that it could contain more meaning than a life lasting eighty years."

There is a difference between living and existing.

Existing is traveling through life on autopilot. Existing is ignoring our conscience. Existing is wanting to be told what to do by people or institutions or conventions. When we are existing, we are not thinking about our actions. We are following others for a sense of belonging and identity. We plod through the drudgery of life, missing out on embracing the present moment rather than choosing to connect to causes, experiences, and people that can give our lives meaning.

Living is embracing life in all its messy glory. Living is recognizing what is and adapting to change. Living is being responsible for the things we can control and looking to transcend ourselves to connect with others. When we are living, we are making choices every moment of every day and realizing that those choices have consequences—good and bad. Sometimes we find ourselves in situations that are outside our control, and even in these circumstances there is meaning to be found. Ultimately, living is about finding the meaning in all circumstances and responding to what life is demanding of us. It is the difference between sitting in the boat and drifting versus taking up the oars and rowing as best we can.

Are you living or existing? What can you do to live life more fully?

Are there ways in which you are following the crowd for a sense of identity and belonging? Can you think of a time you have modified a position, shunned someone, or taken on a cause simply to fit in? What reasons can you think of that make it worthwhile for you to stand up for actions and viewpoints that more accurately reflect your values?

VIKTOR E. FRANKL AND THE SEARCH FOR MEANING

HAPPINESS

"Happiness cannot be pursued; it must ensue, and it only does so as the unintended side effect of one's dedication to a cause greater than oneself or as the by-product of one's surrender to a person other than oneself. Happiness must happen . . . you have to let it happen by not caring about it."

Everyone says they want to be happy. We wish it for our loved ones and ourselves. Harvard's and Yale's curriculums now offer classes on happiness. According to Yale, it is the most popular class in the school's history.

Frankl reminds us that while we think we want to be happy, what we really want is a reason to be happy.

When we make happiness the goal, we establish an unattainable expectation. Happiness, in and of itself, is not a sustainable emotion, because life has ups and downs. Catastrophes, disappointments, and conflicts are as much a part of life as good fortune, success, and harmony.

Frankl describes happiness as a side effect of finding meaning or purpose in life. Happiness occurs when we are least focused on ourselves. It follows in the wake of those times when we give of ourselves to a cause we believe in or to the love of another. Happiness is the reward that ensues when we do something meaningful.

Reflect on a moment when you experienced great happiness.

What were you doing? Was your focus on yourself, someone else, or something else? What were the reasons that
moment made you happy?

VIKTOR E. FRANKL AND THE SEARCH FOR MEANING

REACTIONS

"An abnormal reaction to an abnormal situation is normal behavior."

We often find ourselves focusing on the "abnormal reaction" our mind or body is exhibiting (anxiety, depression, headaches, stomachaches, self-harm, addiction), but such pathologizing fails to put our experiences into context. Often the reaction is completely understandable given the situation.

Our painful reactions are signals that something is not right. Depression is normal when we regularly compare ourselves and our lives to the seemingly perfect bodies and perfect lifestyles we see on social media. Chronic anxiety is normal in the face of constant performance testing, being bombarded with negative news, and answering to relentless deadlines set by others. Often these signals relate to the repression of our spirit's pursuit of meaning or the devaluation of our uniqueness in favor of one-size-fits-all approaches.

We are never free from conditions, but we are free to take a stand, either in the choices we make to change the condition or, when that is not possible, in our attitude toward it.

Reflect on an "abnormal reaction" you are having, perhaps anxiety or depression. What is the situation you are in? What specifically about the situation is contributing to your reaction?

Can you change the situation? If not, how can you change your attitude? Does the change in attitude or situation modify your reaction?

Looking back on your life, have there been times that you have changed your response based on changing your attitude or situation? Why did you choose to change your attitude or situation?

TOLERANCE

"I must be tolerant. This does not mean I share another one's belief. But it does mean that I acknowledge another one's right to believe in and obey his own conscience."

Each one of us is unique—even within our own families, cultures, and religions. While as human beings we are more alike than different, we must acknowledge these differences and the right of other people to have different beliefs and views contrary to our own. The context of our individual lives shapes us, and we can never truly put ourselves in another's shoes. We must try and learn to respect their viewpoint and engage in healthy discourse. It is only when we seek to understand rather than to be understood that we are able to expand our perspectives.

Since tolerance is built on understanding, not judging, seek out someone who holds a view contrary to your own and ask them to explain their position. Rather than thinking about your rebuttal, listen carefully so you can summarize their position in a way that they believe accurately reflects their views. You can begin your summary with, "I'm hearing you say that . . . " and then ask if this is correct. What did you notice about the experience of listening carefully? Ask if they would be willing to reciprocate the practice with you. What did you notice about the experience of being heard?

VIKTOR E. FRANKL AND THE SEARCH FOR MEANING

Make a list of ways you can expand your viewpoints, such as reading a book by an author whose life experience is vastly different from your own or engaging in an activity that allows you to learn about other lifestyles, religions, or political positions.

Take yourself on a field trip that challenges a stereotype or belief you hold. Write down a list of things you learned or observed that surprised you in a positive way. Did you discover any values that were similar to your own? Were your original perceptions confirmed or changed?

VIKTOR E. FRANKL AND THE SEARCH FOR MEANING

COMMUNITY

"The community certainly needs individual personalities –and, indeed, the other way around: every individual personality needs the community in order to find fulfillment within its structure; in other words, to be allowed to become a whole person."

The Masai warriors in Africa greet each other as follows:

"How are the children?"

"All the children are well."

The Masai know that the strength of their community is only as good as the health and well-being of the weakest and most dependent members, usually the children. In every society, children reflect the health of the adults and the community overall.

Our children are not well. On one end, our culture leaves countless children behind in under-resourced schools and communities. On the other end, we place a relentless focus on résumé building for college applications. Either way, our children are left with little time to develop a sense of self, explore interests, and invest in relationships.

Across the board, standardized education and its tests devalue the uniqueness of each human being and miss the multiple levels of human intelligence. This, combined with our children's dependence on social media for validation and personal connection, has undermined their ability to develop a sense of significance and belonging within their communities. Of course, this affects us all. For the first time, we have disbanded our human tribe and are going it alone, which leaves us feeling isolated even in the midst of a sea of humanity.

Human beings need connection, collaboration, and cooperation to flourish. It is how we grow and develop. We need to recognize and respect the relationship between the health of the individuals who make up our communities and the health of our society as a whole, especially our most vulnerable members, like our children.

Reflect on your role in one of the many communities in which you belong (for example, family, work, church, neighborhood, or city). How does your involvement support your connection to others? Could your connections to others help you grow as an individual and enhance your community?

Have you ever had an experience where you met someone or experienced something that sparked an interest or motivated you to get involved? What do you remember about it that was inspirational? Are you still involved? If not, would you be able to reconnect to that activity?

Is there something that you want to see done (big or small) that could positively impact people you care about? Could you start now?

VIKTOR E. FRANKL AND THE SEARCH FOR MEANING

SELF-TRANSCENDENCE

"Being human means always being directed toward something other than oneself.

Even the concept of self-actualization can never do full justice to the main essence of human existence. . . . Human existence is not characterized by self-actualization but rather by what I call self-transcendence— pointing beyond itself."

No man is an island. We are all interconnected, and it is only through others that we become truly fulfilled human beings. This is why self-actualization, by itself, is not enough to help us reach our potential. Self-actualization focuses solely on the improvement of the individual—with the goal of perfecting our *self*.

According to Frankl, this is too limiting. His core belief was that self-transcendence—reaching out beyond ourselves—was the ultimate goal of our existence. We are profoundly social beings, and our lives require interconnection.

Over the course of history, we have been inspired by the unselfish actions of people who have stepped up to address the challenges and needs of their time. Mother Teresa left the comfort of a wealthy family to dedicate herself to those in extreme poverty. On September 11, 2001, as the World Trade Center was burning and collapsing, firefighters and police officers ran up the stairwells to help save those trapped inside. During the global pandemic of 2020, medical professionals, active and retired, made similar sacrifices in the face of exposure to an unknown virus. All these actions epitomize self-transcendence.

The transformative power of moving beyond ourselves is where we find deep satisfaction. This comes from knowing that our lives matter and that we each can have an important role to play in improving our world.

Reflect on your goals and aspirations. Do they involve something or someone other than yourself? How might you modify them to reach self-transcendence? What are a few immediate changes you could make to expand your focus?

Was there a situation where you didn't help someone when you could have and felt bad about it? How could you do something now that would make amends for that missed opportunity?

Write down something you said or did that made a difference in someone else's life today.

BE THE CHANGE

"But the human being is responsible and free and is responsible for his own behavior and conduct and decisions and . . . always . . . retains the freedom to change."

When we stand on the sidelines and critique, without participating in the solution, we usually end up angry and frustrated because we have made ourselves powerless. It is important to remember that we always have the ability to change ourselves, which in turn gives us the power to change our world.

For example, when we decide to improve our health by walking more, going to the gym, or joining a hiking club, we not only improve our physical well-being, but we also change our attitude about ourselves, meet new people, and sometimes inspire someone we care about to do the same.

On a broader scale, if we are mad about the harm being done to the environment, we can engage in activities that benefit the environment. A positive reaction to problems not only changes our personal world but also the world in general.

We have the ability to choose to change ourselves and address the things, big or small, that we don't like in our lives and our world. Instead of delegating responsibility to other people or institutions and then becoming frustrated with them for not solving the problems that concern us, we can follow Gandhi's advice and be the change we wish to see in the world.

Identify a personal or world issue you are concerned about and then identify a change you can make (for at least three weeks) that will help to address the issue. After three weeks, note how your changed attitude or behavior impacted you, those around you, the issue itself, and also your belief in your power to change yourself and your world.

Is there something that you want to see done (big or small) that you have procrastinated about doing that you could start doing this week?

Have you ever had something done to you, either positively or negatively, and then turned around and did the same thing to someone else? If it was positive, describe the experience. If negative, were you able to turn the situation around by doing something positive in response? Would you do it now?

VIKTOR E. FRANKL AND THE SEARCH FOR MEANING

HUMOR

"One might say as well that humor helps man rise above his own predicament by looking at himself in a more detached way.

"So humor would also have to be located in the noetic dimension. After all, no animal is able to laugh, least of all at himself."

As we engage with life, we encounter hurtful and embarrassing moments that cause us to be self-critical or feel shame. We can handle this by becoming cautious and limiting our exposure to possible moments of failure, or we can follow Frankl's advice and use our human ability to detach from ourselves with humor and gain perspective. The problem with the first approach is that when we limit our exposure, we also limit our potential—and our ability to experience the full range of life's joys and opportunities. Viewing our life with humor is essential to accepting our imperfections and coping with life's uncomfortable situations. Laughing at our low moments encourages us to forgive ourselves and allows us the vulnerability we need to deeply connect with others.

Talented comedians are excellent observers of the human condition and turn universally embarrassing moments into shared moments of laughter. Often the people we enjoy most are those who can laugh at their own mistakes or flaws and allow other people to laugh with them. We connect more through our imperfections than our perfections. When we develop our uniquely human skill of self-distancing with humor, we are better able to face our challenges and enjoy life.

Reflect on an embarrassing moment in your life. Step back and put it in perspective. Turn it into a funny story. Tell it to yourself. Tell it to someone else. Notice how it feels to use humor to heal.

When was the last time you made someone laugh, either purposefully or accidentally? How did that affect the situation or your relationship with that person?

Have you ever used humor to face challenges in your own life? How did it affect the outcome?

VIKTOR E. FRANKL AND THE SEARCH FOR MEANING

UNIQUENESS

"The meaning of life must be conceived in terms of the specific meaning of a personal life in a given situation. Each man is unique, after all, and each man's life is singular; no one is replaceable nor is his life repeatable."

We are so much more than the combined DNA of our parents or the products of our environment. We are each as distinct as our fingerprints; even identical twins have different fingerprints!

Every one of us has something to contribute to the world. Our contributions stem not only from our perfections but also from our imperfections. A 2019 study showed 35 percent of US entrepreneurs are dyslexic. Dyslexia, classified as a learning disability, is in fact what gives these entrepreneurs their unique ability to problem solve—they see the world in a different light.

What makes us unique and different is often what gives us an advantage. Our distinct makeup is composed of our talents and flaws, our strengths and weaknesses, as well as our experiences, whether they are positive or negative. All these things make us unique and irreplaceable.

Consider what makes you unique. What do you view as your talents, strengths, and positive experiences? What do you view as your handicaps, weaknesses, and challenging experiences? In what ways can you use your unique characteristics and experiences to help others or causes you care about?

Identify one or more people you know or know of and describe the characteristics that make them unique and irreplaceable.

In what way have they made a contribution to your life or the world? Were they always popular and accepted? Do you think they mainly focused on how they were perceived by others? Do you share any of the same qualities? If not, are there any you would like to incorporate into your life?

VIKTOR E. FRANKL AND THE SEARCH FOR MEANING

HUMANITY

"We are . . . not always fully aware of all those under-privileged people, underdeveloped populations, and so forth. And if you were aware of it, life would again become meaningful. [There are] a lot of tasks in wait for us all. We would just have to make another step after having arrived and developed what is called mono-theism, the belief in the one God. [We] should also obtain what I would like to call the 'monoanthropism,' the awareness of the one mankind . . . a unity of man-kind which goes beyond all different colors, be it colors of the skin or colors . . . of the various political parties."

While we are all individuals, we also share a common humanity. At certain moments in time, we are especially aware of this. When Neil Armstrong first stepped on the moon, the world stopped to watch in awe as he proclaimed, "That's one small step for man, one giant leap for mankind." It was a unifying moment of joy. Similarly, pandemics, mass murders, and natural disasters unite us in grief and sorrow. It is in these moments that we recognize each other as fellow human beings and are able to focus more on our commonalities than our differences.

We share the same planet. Wars and strife in one region generate migration patterns that affect other regions; disease and pollution in one part of the world eventually travel to other parts of the world. Caring for each other and our planet is essential to our health and well-being. What happens to one of us eventually affects us all.

When we step outside ourselves and choose to get involved, we often discover what we have in common with the people we want to support and causes we want to assist. When we shift our focus from ourselves to the world around us, we often find contentment, fulfillment, and purpose.

Think of someone that you feel is very different from yourself (maybe even the same person you spoke with for reflection five) and identify views and/or values that you have in common. How does this shift your opinion of that person? What actions might flow from this broadened perspective?

Describe a time in your life when you found common meaning with another person or a group of people. Did this change a stranger or an opponent into an ally?

What do you think about Frankl's view of humanity as one mankind?

VIKTOR E. FRANKL AND THE SEARCH FOR MEANING

FREEDOM

"Man is by no means fully free. Man is not free from determinants. Man's freedom is a finite freedom, not freedom from conditions; his freedom lies in the potentiality for taking a stand toward whatever conditions might confront him."

If anyone had a reason to carry a grudge, it would have been Viktor Frankl. He was the survivor of four Nazi concentration camps and lost his parents, brother, wife, and unborn child in the Holocaust. Despite these horrific events, he chose not to be consumed by hatred and blame. Instead, he often said he would not forget any good deed done to him nor would he carry a grudge for a bad deed.

Logotherapy focuses on choice, even if it is only the choice of the attitude we take in a situation of unavoidable suffering. Sadly, tragedy can befall anyone at any time. It can present itself in the form of wars, disasters, crimes, or disease. Our freedom comes in how we respond to each personal crisis that confronts us. By identifying as victims, we are prevented from identifying as survivors. To be controlled by anger and to insist on blame renders us powerless. When we consciously choose how we respond, we regain control and power over our future. We cannot change the past. We can only learn from it and decide who we want to be as we responsibly move forward.

Is there a situation in your life that makes you feel like a victim or trapped by your fears? Can you retell the story to yourself, casting yourself as courageous, empowered, or as a survivor? How does it feel to play that role? Moving forward, what thoughts and actions will allow you to shift the focus from "what was" to "what can be meaningful"?

Describe how someone you know has turned their personal tragedy into something meaningful. Have you ever done the same? If so, describe one of those times.

Have you ever forgiven someone who did something hurtful to you? What made you decide to forgive them?

MONEY

"Man is afraid of his inner void, of the existential vacuum, and runs away into work or into pleasure. The place of his frustrated will to meaning is taken by the will to power, even though it be just economic power, financial power, that is to say the most primitive form of the will to power: the will to money."

Frankl used the term "will to money" to refer to the focus on the pursuit of money as the primary driver of a person's life. Our culture reveres the wealthy. We view wealth as the solution to all problems and as the creator of status, belonging, and respect. Our corporations and our education systems make upward financial mobility the goal.

It is not money itself that is the problem, as it can actually make a positive impact in the world. The issue is how we view money and what we do with it. If we focus on acquiring wealth beyond our basic needs, it can lose its value of enhancing our life by consuming our time and energy. Money can buy things, but it cannot buy love, happiness, or fulfillment.

Our society encourages us to live our lives according to what author David Brooks calls "résumé virtues"—accomplishments and financial rewards that we feel set us apart from everyone else. But study after study shows that it is our "eulogy virtues"—deep relationships, community contributions, and meaningful work—that we are most remembered for and that give us fulfillment in life.

Keep a log for a week, noting how you spend your time (sleep, work, friends, significant others, family, hobbies, and so forth). Are you spending time on the things you value and want to be remembered for? If not, what shifts could you make in time and/or attention to focus on eulogy virtues?

What role does money play in your life? Is it a means to an end or an accumulation for power and status? What other things could you do with money?

Have you ever been to a funeral where the eulogy was really inspiring? Did you rethink your own life based on what you heard?

EMPTINESS

"It is the very problem of our time that people are caught by a pervasive feeling of meaninglessness. . . . It is accompanied by a feeling of emptiness. . . . The 'existential vacuum' . . . has increased and spread literally all over the world. Our industrialized society is out to satisfy all needs, and our consumer society is even out to create needs in order to satisfy them; but the most human of all human needs—the need to see a meaning in one's life—remains unsatisfied."

Frankl expressed concern over our industrialized systems, noting that people are not machines and that to treat them as such would lead to an existential vacuum (a feeling of emptiness) often resulting in depression, aggression, and addiction. As early as 1928, he developed counseling centers in response to students in Vienna who were committing suicide around the time report cards were issued. Frankl got students to identify meaningful goals for their future rather than hyper-focusing on their immediate academic performance. The suicide rate dropped.

The education system seeks to conform students to an external standard that is often not meaningful to them, resulting in boredom (lack of interest) and apathy (lack of motivation). Even after people complete their schooling, the pattern of pursuing goals set by others continues—meeting career goals set by employers, commitment expectations set by community and religious organizations, as well as social expectations set by peers. These externally imposed benchmarks often overwhelm us, leaving us with little time to think about or pursue things that matter to us.

When we ignore our individuality and our need to discover our unique meaning and purpose for living, we are left feeling empty. By critically evaluating whether or not external benchmarks are in line with our personal values and goals, we are empowered to live a meaningful life.

Are you hyper-focused on your performance, or do you feel empty inside? If so, identify at least one personal goal you can work toward that will positively impact your life.

Are you searching for things that are meaningful, or are you allowing others to determine your daily activities? Are there any reasons why you would change that?

Do you mostly listen to your conscience, or do you tend to avoid unpleasant situations and follow "the path of least resistance"?

VIKTOR E. FRANKL AND THE SEARCH FOR MEANING

RESPONSIBILITY

"Man is responsible for the fulfillment of the specific meaning of his personal life. But he is also responsible before something, or to something, be it society, or humanity, or mankind, or his own conscience."

Our ability to choose what we do in life is what gives us our freedom. Frankl repeatedly emphasized that we are not free from conditions, but we are always free to choose how we respond to them. Because we are free, we are responsible for who we become and how we address the issues that impact our families, communities, and the world.

Although we cannot control the limitations that biology and circumstances place on us, we can decide how they will influence our lives. What makes us unique is also what makes us uniquely capable of improving situations or the lives of others. We must put our energy, talent, and experience toward positively contributing to the issues that call to us, whether that means curing diseases, helping foster youth, or solving world hunger. It is only when we recognize that our freedom comes with responsibility that we can improve the quality of our lives and the state of the world. Life doesn't just happen to us. As Frankl says, we have to play an active role in making life meaningful.

Exercise the freedom that comes with responsibility by looking at any problem of concern to you (personal, communal, or global). Identify at least two ways that you can respond. After noting the likely outcomes and how they align with your values, decide how to respond. How does consciously deciding how to respond make you feel?

Identify the things in your life that you are responsible for, both in terms of the people you help and the tasks you undertake. Are you doing more than is beneficial for them? If so, why?

HUMAN SPIRIT

"Man's search for a meaning is not pathological but rather the surest sign of being truly human. Even if this search is frustrated, it cannot be considered a sign of disease. It is spiritual distress, not mental disease."

Our human spirit is never sick. It can become distressed and manifest itself outwardly in ailments that affect our bodies and/or minds. We often want to see these things as psychological or biological problems so we can label them with a diagnosis and attempt to find a cure. This approach reduces us to only a mind and body and ignores the spiritual dimension that is the essence of our humanity.

Our spiritual dimension is what provides us with the resources and strength we need to move forward in our lives. These resources include:

- our ability to learn from our mistakes, allowing us to adapt to new circumstances

- our sense of humor, putting our failings into perspective
- our conscience, giving us the ability to take a stand for things we believe in or against things we think are wrong
- our ability to love others, helping us move beyond ourselves
- our passion for a cause, allowing us the potential to create change in the world

The search for meaning is a deeply personal and spiritual journey. No person or system can determine what is meaningful for us or define what will give our lives purpose. Because our culture is driven by external benchmarks (wealth, power, individual achievement, everlasting youth, physical perfection) that keep us perpetually busy, we often find ourselves on a treadmill that robs us of the time and energy required to discover what life is asking of our human spirit. We need to look at whether what we call *disease* (or *dis*-ease) is really our spirit crying out in distress.

Is your body or mind signaling something to you? Rather than being a psychological or biological issue, could this signal be related to the suppression of your human spirit? If you had to guess, what is your spirit longing for?

Can you think of a time when you made a mistake and learned from it? How did you choose to apply your new-found knowledge?

Do you feel like you are on a treadmill that makes it difficult for you to hear and respond to what your conscience is guiding you toward? Do you find yourself so busy that you don't have time to think about what life is asking of you? What do you do in these moments?

VIKTOR E. FRANKL AND THE SEARCH FOR MEANING

TENSION

"Thus, it can be seen that mental health is based on a certain degree of tension, the tension between what one has already achieved and what one still ought to accomplish, or the gap between what one is and what one should become. Such a tension is inherent in the human being and therefore is indispensable to mental well-being."

In order to grow and change, we need tension between what we are and what we want to become. While we might desire equilibrium in our body (with sleep and nutrition) and our mind (with stable emotions), seeking this is not always healthy for our spirit. When equilibrium is the goal, we are likely to stick with what is comfortable and familiar, thus limiting our opportunities for growth.

Tension has to be present in our spirit in order to propel us forward. Striving toward a goal, addressing the issues that arise in relationships, developing new skills, making new friends, and even falling in love can cause tension. All these things challenge our equilibrium. Luckily, our human spirit provides us with the resources we need to handle these situations. Only when we embrace the tension that comes with living can we fulfill our potential and become who we are meant to be.

Do you feel like you are struggling to reach a goal, create a project, or connect in a relationship? What is the tension between who you are and who you'd like to become? How can you turn this tension into fuel to help push you toward achieving your dreams?

VIKTOR E. FRANKL AND THE SEARCH FOR MEANING

Describe a time when you felt compelled to do something about a situation you found yourself in. Did your decision to respond cause you tension? What did you learn or discover from the experience?

Do you think it is possible to live a meaningful life without experiencing tension? If your goal is to avoid adversity or stress, what kind of legacy do you think you would leave behind?

Think of important turning points in your life (e.g., changing jobs or moving to a new city). How did you cope with these? How did your responses change the way you lived your life going forward?

VIKTOR E. FRANKL AND THE SEARCH FOR MEANING

SOLITUDE

"No situation repeats itself, and each situation calls for a different response. Sometimes the situation in which a man finds himself may require him to shape his own fate by action. At other times it is more advantageous for him to make use of an opportunity for contemplation."

The distractions of our modern society provide us with the opportunity to keep our minds occupied around the clock. Whether by streaming videos, checking emails, or engaging with social media, our busyness keeps us from listening to the human spirit within us—the conscience that guides us.

It is only when we slow down and reflect on our life that we can gain perspective. When we are alone and quiet, we can contemplate who we want to be and where we want to go. By contrast, when we are racing from one thing to another, keeping ourselves perpetually busy, we have to evaluate if we are running to something or from something. Often, we are running from loneliness, but loneliness is a part of being human. In fact, solitude is essential for reflecting on what matters to us and formulating our plans for the future.

As we go through life's inevitable ups and downs—with work or relationship transitions, social circle evolutions, and the death of friends or loved ones—we experience loneliness. In our culture, loneliness can generate depression and anxiety, and often feels shameful. But we should also remember that loneliness is usually temporary and that it is during these periods of struggle that we grow the most.

Take a few minutes a day to sit with yourself. You can use this time to contemplate or meditate. This can be as simple as focusing on your breath and quieting your mind. Note how creating time for quiet solitude affects how you feel and how you react to things.

Do you regularly take time for solitude and contemplation? How much time do you spend? Do you think you spend too much time or too little? Do you find the practice helpful?

For a couple of days, write down what comes to mind during your quiet time. Is there a theme or consistent message?

Does solitude make you uncomfortable? If so, why? Could there be something you are trying to avoid? How might acknowledging it help you address it?

VIKTOR E. FRANKL AND THE SEARCH FOR MEANING

SUFFERING

"If there is a meaning in life at all, then there must be a meaning in suffering. Suffering is an ineradicable part of life, even as fate and death. Without suffering and death, human life cannot be complete."

While positive psychology certainly has its merits, it ignores suffering, which is an inescapable part of life. Psychologist Susan David calls this the "tyranny of positivity," as it creates an unrealistic expectation and generates shame when we have feelings that are not positive. Negative emotions are a natural part of being alive and allow us to experience the healthy range of human experience. We must remember we always have the power to address our suffering with a change in our situation, or when that is not possible, a change in our attitude.

To experience great joy, we also must risk experiencing great pain. We must develop the ability to appreciate the highs and cope with the lows. When we run from suffering rather than accept the reality of its existence, we give it power over our lives and lose the opportunities for personal growth that it presents. To really live, we must be willing to experience the full range of emotions that come with being human.

What is your view of suffering? Is it something you avoid or accept? Looking back on a time of suffering, can you see personal growth that came from the situation? Based on this experience, identify healthy coping strategies you can use in the future.

Think of someone you admire and describe how they handled a difficult situation well (illness, death of a loved one, etc.). What made you think they handled the situation well? Can you identify what they did that you could apply if you find yourself in a difficult situation?

Think of a time of crisis in your life. Looking back on it, are you now grateful for the challenge. How did it help you grow?

WORK

"At the same time, an appeal is made to our responsibility—precisely to bring what has not yet happened *into* the world! And each of us must do this as part of our daily work, as part of our everyday lives. So everyday life becomes the reality per se, and this reality becomes the potential for action."

How work fits into our lives is largely dependent on how we view ourselves in relation to our job. When we disconnect our work from who we are and what we value, we lead a divided life. In this context of compartmentalization, the so-called work-life balance limits our potential to bring our unique contributions to all our interactions.

We have the freedom to choose how we invest ourselves in all aspects of our lives, including work. This allows us to find meaning in all that we do. If we view our work as an extension of our connection to inner meaning, work becomes integrated into our lives in a more profound way. The term work-life balance becomes more about time spent at different pursuits, not energy drained away from competing core pursuits.

For example, a nurse can strictly follow a doctor's medical orders, committing to procedure without engaging with a patient on an emotional level. Alternatively, the nurse can follow procedure while connecting with the patient through empathy and compassion. The second approach, where the nurse reaches out emotionally within the framework of expected duties, brings meaning through work.

Every occupation allows us to give of ourselves in a way that engages who we are, with our unique insights, understanding, genetics, and experiences. When these complex parts of our identities are put to work in a meaningful, purposeful way, we become indispensable and irreplaceable.

How does your work relate to your life? Do you find it meaningful or does it help you achieve personal goals? What aspects of who you are and what you have experienced can you incorporate into your work to make it more meaningful?

VIKTOR E. FRANKL AND THE SEARCH FOR MEANING

Is what you are doing with your work the most meaning-ful use of your time? Do you feel called to do something different? If so, what?

Broadening your view of work to include the basic responsibilities you take on in your daily life (such as cleaning, cooking, caretaking, etc.), can you think of someone or something you care about that makes the chore meaningful? Thinking of your "why," does it make you approach the activity differently?

CHOICES

"I prefer to live in a world in which man has the right to make choices, albeit wrong choices, rather than a world in which no choice at all is left to him."

Every day we are confronted with a multitude of demands and choices. The demands we meet and the choices we make will, over the course of our lives, define the type of person we are.

Viktor Frankl did not fear getting older or dying, because he viewed life as an opportunity to do things that mattered and to consciously make choices that were meaningful. With each meaningful choice he built up a past that he could look back on with satisfaction—a past that was permanently part of who he was. Frankl's focus was on the fullness of life, not its length.

If we take the time to think about how we want to be remembered, we might make totally different—and likely better—decisions about how to spend our time now. As we move forward in life, we are building a permanent past. By embracing the gift of each day and consciously engaging in the things we do, we can put the majority of our time and energy into things we consider important. Since we only live once, the choices we make matter.

Do you sometimes feel that you are stretching yourself too thin fulfilling all the meaningful tasks in your life? How do you respond to the moment-to-moment situations demanding your attention? Are there any situations in which you are irreplaceable? How do you make choices about which ones are the highest priority?

Are you building a past that you can look back on with satisfaction? What are some key moments where your choices made a difference in your life or the lives of others?

Make a list of meaningful choices you have made.

Looking back at the themes you identified during times of solitude and contemplation, are there any changes you plan to make going forward?

Make a list of meaningful choices you hope to make in the future.

ACKNOWLEDGMENTS

This book would not have been possible without the invaluable support, encouragement, and input of Alexander Vesely-Frankl, Viktor Frankl's grandson, who is a certified logotherapist. He reviewed the questions, narrative, and prompts to make sure they were true to his grandfather's message. Alexander and his father, Franz Vesely, provided us with a multitude of resources from the family archives. We are grateful to the Frankl family and to the Viktor Frankl Institute of Vienna for their indispensable assistance with the creation of this book.

SOURCES

The quotes in this book are from the following six works by Viktor E. Frankl:

Embracing Hope: On Freedom, Responsibility & the Meaning of Life. Boston: Beacon Press, 2024.

The Feeling of Meaninglessness: A Challenge to Psychotherapy and Philosophy. Milwaukee: Marquette University Press, 2010.

Man's Search for Meaning. Boston: Beacon Press, 2019.

San Quentin Lecture Transcript, Frankl Family Archives, 1966.

Yes to Life: In Spite of Everything. Boston: Beacon Press, 2020.

Youth in Search of Two Worlds Symposium, Sacramento State College Speech (audio tape), Frankl Family Archives, 1966.

MORE INFORMATION

Learn more about the life and work of Viktor Frankl on our website. We offer resources and information about Viktor Frankl and logotherapy, and his meaning-centered approach to therapy and life. The website includes a personal biography, a summary of logotherapy, video clips, books, films, and news articles.

Find us at:

VIKTORFRANKLAMERICA.COM

Additional resources can be found through the Viktor Frankl Institute, Vienna:

VIKTORFRANKL.ORG

BOOKS BY VIKTOR FRANKL

Man's Search for Meaning
(Beacon Press, 2019)

Yes to Life: In Spite of Everything
(Beacon Press, 2020)

Embracing Hope: On Freedom,
Responsibility & the Meaning of Life
(Beacon Press, 2024)

ABOUT THE AUTHORS

ABOUT PAM ROY

PAM ROY is a writer, filmmaker, investor, and philanthropist with a mission to provide community-based support for youth and families. Inspired by the meaning-oriented philosophy of Viktor Frankl, she is involved in film and book projects related to bringing his ideas to a new generation. Pam cofounded the Viktor E. Frankl Institute of America (VFIA) with Frankl's grandson, Alexander Vesely-Frankl, and Moira Hummel. It provides resources related to meaning-centered theory and philosophy. She co-authored *The Inspiring Wisdom of Viktor E. Frankl: A 21-Day Reflection Book About Meaning* with Moira and developed a course with Alexander called Viktor Frankl's Logotherapy: The Discovery of Meaning (offered on the VFIA website and Udemy). She is an executive producer of the forthcoming feature film adaption of the international best-selling book *Man's Search for Meaning*.

Pam is also the cofounder of Straight Up Impact (a women-owned production company focused on social change) and B-Unbound (an initiative with Big Picture Learning that connects youth with community-based mentors who share their interests). She is the author of *Parenting from the Passenger Seat: How Our Children Develop Capabilities, Connections, and Meaningful Lives*, which supports parents in helping children navigate their own way.

In addition, Pam serves on the advisory board of the Friendship Bench, a program that trains grandmothers to treat depression. She is producing a feature film related to *The Friendship Bench* inspired by

Dixon Chibanda's TED talk and was an executive producer of a documentary about the program. Her volunteer involvement with foster youth and survivors of human trafficking expresses her deep commitment to community service. Lastly, Pam is co-owner of Vaca Restaurant with Ahmed Labbate and Chef Amar Santana.

ABOUT MOIRA HUMMEL

MOIRA HUMMEL's career began as a civil litigation attorney specializing in research and writing. In 2015, she shifted her focus to pursuing her dream of working with children and young adults in foster care. For over a decade, Moira worked with several nonprofits assisting foster youth at sibling reunification camps and in life-skills training programs. She continues to act as a mentor for individual foster youth and to support organizations serving this community. For the last twenty years, she has been a volunteer and board member of Brothers' Helpers, a nonprofit that feeds the poor and the homeless in Los Angeles County. More recently, she has started working with churches and other nonprofits to create places for people to find and build community.

Moira read *Man's Search for Meaning* and became convinced that Frankl's life philosophy has the potential to transform lives. For several years she was the content editor for *Pam Roy Blog*, a blog that incorporated Viktor Frankl's teachings and life philosophy into its insights and advice on education and parenting issues. Moira cofounded the Viktor Frankl Institute of America with Pam Roy and Alexander Vesely-Frankl. She is involved with helping to build programs that will incorporate Viktor Frankl's teachings and life philosophy into community-based organizations and nonprofits.